BLESSINGS
of a
FATHER

BLESSINGS *of a* FATHER

RANDY BROWN

CREATION
HOUSE
A STRANG COMPANY

BLESSINGS OF A FATHER by Randy Brown
Published by Creation House
A Strang Company
600 Rinehart Road
Lake Mary, Florida 32746
www.creationhouse.com

Unless otherwise noted, all Scripture quotations are from the King James Version of the Bible.

Cover design by Terry Clifton

Library of Congress Control Number: 2005939103
International Standard Book Number: 1-59185-997-2

First Edition

06 07 08 09 10—987654321
Printed in the United States of America

Contents

Foreword

GOD CALLS PEOPLE who are reverent to His name, fervent in spirit, and willing to say, "Yes, Lord." One such individual who has heeded the call is Apostle Randy Brown. It is my privilege and honor to know him as my spiritual son and servant of the most high God. The ministry both he and his wife, Pastor Gayle, share is a unique combination of leadership and servitude. The love they shower upon their congregation at Bread of Life Fellowship reaches beyond the four walls of a building to all nations.

The anointing upon this ministry is evident not only in the pulpit but in the pages of this book. Your life will be transformed as you study this mighty word.

BECAUSE HE LIVES,
PASTOR GENE PROFETA

Chapter 1

The Birth Blessing

THE FOLLOWING INFORMATION is intended to build up your spirit and cause your life to go through stirrings and changes. I truly believe there are blessings designated for a father to impart to his children. These are blessings a father can release from his spirit, from his overseer/headship position (if you would like to call it that), into the lives of his children to be able to send them into realms of success and prosperity, blessings, guidance, and breakthroughs. In order for his children's lives to be orchestrated so that positive change can take place, I believe the father must be involved in their lives.

A funny thing used to happen to me as I was growing up. Every morning as my brother, sisters, and I were preparing for school, we would hear the voice of my dad at the bottom of the staircase. He would shout, "Get up! Get up! It is gonna be a great day. Get up! Get up! It is gonna be a great day." Now, as a young man not wanting to get up and go to school, to me this was an irritation. I did not understand the spiritual positioning and the greatness of the manifestation of God behind all of it; so to me it became an irritation.

To embrace it in its revelatory realm, from my childhood years through my teen years my dad was setting a platform of spiritual existence for me, which has manifested in my life even today. He projected from his spirit into my life: "Today is gonna be great." He never once told me today was bad; he never once let the weather deter him from his statements. It could be snowing, raining, sunny, or stormy; it could be winter, spring, summer, or fall, but every morning when he got to the bottom of that staircase he would begin to shout out, "Get up! Get up! It is gonna be a great day."

Though I was a child born-again and loving the Lord, I couldn't embrace it because of my desire not to get up to go to school. Thanks be to God, however, that my spirit embraced the revelation of the speech of my dad and it caused me (I believe) to escalate and expand into realms that I am in now, and which I will be going into in the days to come.

> And they journeyed from Bethel; and there was but a little way to come to Ephrath: and Rachel travailed, and she had hard labour. And it came to pass, when she was in hard labour, that the midwife said unto her, Fear not; thou shalt have this son also. And it came to pass, as her soul was in departing, (for she died) that she called his name Benoni: but his father called him Benjamin. And Rachel died, and was buried in the way to Ephrath, which is Bethlehem.
>
> —GENESIS 35:16–19

Now this is a tremendous example of a blessing released from a father onto a child. There are several types of blessings I want to address in this book, but the first one is the birth blessing. I believe a daddy needs to bless his children at birth, upon their coming into the world.

During Rachel's hardship of delivery she called out the boy's name, Benoni. The name *Benoni* means "you have brought me sorrow" or "your days shall be filled with sorrow" or "you shall be sorrowful." This is what Rachel voiced upon the child's beginnings. A child's beginning is very important to the course and direction of his/her life. Rachel voiced this upon her son's life because of her suffering; perhaps she even knew she was dying. But the daddy, Jacob, said his name will not be Benoni, but shall be *Benjamin*. *Benjamin* means "the son of my right hand" or "the son of power and authority." On the right hand of God there is power and authority; I believe this was a great impartation.

Jacob was setting up his son's beginnings, his launchings, his starting place. He wasn't letting him be lukewarm, he wasn't letting him be staggered, he wasn't letting him start broken but gave his beginning a great name. He called him Benjamin. He was setting up his son's life to be great from the giddy up. At Benjamin's birth, Jacob declared, *Your name is even great that you shall be at the right hand of power. You shall be a man of power and a man of authority.* He determined his son would not have a sorrowful or miserable life! He set his foundations, launchings, and beginnings in a motion of success.

A solid, settled, organized starting place was given to this child. That is what a daddy should do: make the beginnings of his child rich and fruitful; not scattered, chaotic, confusing, miserable, and not messed up, but successful, blessed, and prosperous, going forward in the power and things of the Lord. The beginnings of the child's life must be sure! That is where the daddy comes in. He is saying to his child: I am blessing you from your beginnings, blessing you from the beginnings of your natural birth; I am blessing you from the beginnings of your spiritual birth once you are born-again; I am blessing you from the beginning of your projects in life, I am blessing you in your beginning of college days, I am blessing you in your beginning business, I am blessing the beginnings of your new home, I am blessing your beginnings that they just cause a continual effect of the releasing of the goodness of the Lord in your life here in the land of the living.

Genesis 1:1 says, "In the beginning God created the heaven and the earth." I believe the Father is causing the beginnings to have creative presence. The heavenly Father brought about creative presence in the earth and the heavens from the beginning of time. Likewise, a natural father can bring about a creative presence. In his birth blessing the father is saying to his child, you are not going to be sick, diseased, and afflicted; you are not going to be tormented; you are not going to be demon-possessed, drug-addicted or ravaged by alcoholism. You shall be successful because your natural father, walking here on the earth, is a spiritual man in Christ Jesus and is speaking over your life that it will be fruitful, successful, and blessed.

The Book of Job says, "Though thy beginning was small, yet thy latter end should greatly increase" (Job 8:7). Though your child will start off small, as a daddy you must believe the end of your child's life shall be greater than the beginning. Your child might just be in kindergarten now, or junior college, or he may have a job making just twenty thousand dollars a year right now, but his end shall be greater than his beginning. Proclaim this over your child: greatness is coming. Not "greatness is possibly coming" or "greatness maybe hopefully will come," no, say, *Greatness is*

4

coming to my child. He shall be more prosperous at the end than he was at the beginning. Your child's beginnings may have been difficult, the doctors may thought that your child would not make it until he was born. Perhaps your child was born with a disability, a handicap, or a condition in his body, in his blood, or in his life—even though the beginning was difficult, your child's ending shall be great.

The Bible states: "Though thy beginning was small..." (Job 8:7). Do not despise the beginning whether it is small, difficult, or minute; the ending shall be great in volume and in size.

Job 8:8 says, "For enquire, I pray thee, of the former age, and prepare thyself to search of their fathers." See, I want to know that my father released something; I need to know what Dad said over me. You may look back and realize that your father spoke nothing over you. In that case, you need to find a spiritual father. You need somebody to speak into your life and give you instruction and direction. Someone to say, "Go forth!" Someone to say, "Stretch out!" Someone to say, "Explode, expand, enlarge your camp, enlarge your boundaries, enlarge your life, enlarge your settings!" You need someone who will stretch you like that. Keep in mind, however, what your father spoke over you in your beginnings.

> (For we are but of yesterday, and know nothing, because our days upon earth are a shadow:) Shall not they teach thee, and tell thee, and utter words out of their heart? Can the rush grow up without mire? Can the flag grow without water? Whilst it is yet in his greenness, and not cut down, it withereth before any other herb. So are the paths of all that forget God; and the hypocrite's hope shall perish.
>
> —Job 8:9–13

This passage is discussing the fact that everything needs something. Plants need water, and the rush needs the mire. Likewise, children need their father. I wish every father was a godly man and spirit-filled. A spirit-filled daddy speaking and invoking blessings, directions, and instruction into his child's life will cause that child to be greater than what they are at their beginning. With his words of edification the father can send the child into realms of success. When the child tells his father that he (the child) is not doing well, the spirit-filled father is going to say, "You can do well." The child says, "I am not feeling well." The father answers, "You will feel well."

"I am losing my business."

"Your business shall be multiplied and become greater."

"I am losing my house."

"You will buy several more houses and you won't lose this one, either."

The dad's spiritual presence is to push and drive his child from his/her beginning to greatness in life. The child's beginnings will manifest into realms of greatness, break-throughs, overtakings, and going forth by the Spirit of the Living God.

Sometimes we fight through things on a continual basis. We are fighting through one issue, then we are fighting through another. We are fighting through our education, we are fighting through our relationships, we are fighting through our financial situation, we are fighting through our business realms, we are fighting through family crisis, we are fighting through emotional upheaval. We are constantly fighting through life. I believe we have to do a lot of this fighting because our beginnings were unsettled and unstable because there was no daddy helping to set the direction of our life.

People may argue that a mother should be sufficient for filling in this need. Indeed, a mother is a great blessing. The Bible says the mother is the lawgiver (Prov. 1:8). A mother speaks into her child's life and provides the law that will help mold and shape her child. But the Bible also says the father brings instruction (Prov. 1:8). A father is not speaking to mold and shape the child's life. What he speaks must be done; you will succeed! You will do great!

The important point is for the father to release those blessings to impact the beginnings of his children's lives, the beginnings of their education, the beginning of their new house, and the beginning of their business ventures. A child needs the presence and blessings of his/her father in what, where, and how their life will develop so that can experience greatness on a continual basis.

Proverbs 8:22 says, "The LORD possessed me in the beginning of his way, before his works of old." I believe this is an important scripture. The beginnings of your ways need to be possessed by God. Your starting point needs the blessings of God on it. Just because we are born does not mean the blessings of God are upon everything we do. We need to get a hold of a blessing. You can ask the Lord to bless you, and He will bless you. Your pastor can bless you, and you will be blessed. Your job can bless you with a raise, and you will be blessed. Your bank can bless you with a new interest rate, and you will be blessed. But your daddy can bless you and cause you to be possessed with the blessings of God from the beginning of your situation. His blessings will not be on you slightly, they won't touch your life just a little bit. Your father's blessings will actually cause you to

7

be under the control, influence, dominion, omnipresence, and omnipotence of God from your beginnings and into the days to come.

The Lord wants to bless you, and that is what a daddy alone can do in his role. A good, spirit-filled daddy, whether a natural daddy or a spiritual daddy (the pastor, the apostle, the bishop that is overseeing you, your elder) as they speak into your life they can bless you. These blessings of God will possess you and take you higher and higher and higher into where God wants you to be.

I started the writing of this book because every morning my dad stood at the bottom of the staircase and said, "GET UP! GET UP! IT IS GONNA BE A GREAT DAY." So you and your beginning of each day and your beginning of each project, I believe would like some encouragement. A godly father operating in Bible principles can be a great help. My encouragement to my natural children and to my spiritual children is to get them to reach higher. Wherever they may be now they can always do greater. Today will be a great day.

Chapter 2

Birthright Blessing

THERE ARE DIFFERENT kinds of blessings a father can release upon his children. I feel as we look at them we'll realize the importance of spiritual parenting, and that the purpose of the kingdom is the mentoring process by not only fathers, but by mothers as well. Let's look at the birthright blessing:

> And he came unto his father, and said, My father: and he said, Here am I; who art thou, my son? And Jacob said unto his father, I am Esau thy first born; I have done according as thou badest me: arise, I pray thee, sit and eat of my venison, that thy soul may bless me. And Isaac said unto his son, How is it that thou hast found it so quickly, my son? And he said, Because the LORD thy God brought it to me. And Isaac said unto Jacob, Come near, I pray thee, that I may feel thee, my son, whether thou be my very son Esau or not. And Jacob went near unto Isaac his father; and he felt him, and said, The voice is Jacob's voice, but the hands are the hands of Esau. And he discerned him not, because his hands were hairy, as his brother Esau's hands: so he blessed him. And he said, Art thou my very son Esau? And he said, I am. And he said, Bring it near to me, and I will

eat of my son's venison, that my soul may bless thee.
And he brought it near to him, and he did eat: and
he brought him wine and he drank. And his father
Isaac said unto him, Come near now, and kiss me,
my son. And he came near, and kissed him: and he
smelled the smell of his raiment, and blessed him,
and said, See, the smell of my son is as the smell of
a field which the LORD hath blessed: Therefore God
give thee of the dew of heaven, and the fatness of the
earth, and plenty of corn and wine: Let people serve
thee, and nations bow down to thee: be lord over
thy brethren, and let thy mother's sons bow down
to thee: cursed be every one that curseth thee, and
blessed be he that blesseth thee.

—GENESIS 27:18–29

This word from Isaac is powerful. We even hear some
of the Genesis 12 revelatory information as far as bless
them that bless thee or curse them that curse thee that God
spoke to Abraham. This is a presentation, declaration, and a
proclamation of the spirit that is released from a father unto
a firstborn male child. A male child was greatly desired
because the firstborn male child was holy unto God (Exod.
13:2; Luke 2:23).

Now, Jacob's mother assisted him in manipulating the
situation, deceiving his father Isaac, and actually obtain-
ing the birthright blessing. His mother remembered what
God had showed her when she was pregnant; that the elder
would serve the younger (Gen. 25:23). Verses 28–29 say,
"Therefore God give thee of the dew of heaven, and the fatness of the earth, and plenty of corn and wine: Let people
serve thee." Now that is powerful! This birthright blessing
was not just saying that hopefully your life will work out.

This blessing put Jacob in the position of complete rulership, headship, and leadership over the people. People were going to bow down to Jacob, as he would be lord over his brethren. This means that all of Jacob's other family members were beneath him.

Then it says, "Let thy mother's sons bow down to thee" (v. 29). This means any brothers you have, whether half or full brother, they have to bow down to you if they're from your mother. You will be above and beyond them. Then it goes on to say, "Cursed be everyone that curseth thee, and blessed be he that blesseth thee" (v. 29). This puts you in a protective mode knowing that no weapon formed against you can prosper and that anyone who wishes evil or curses you will be cursed. (See Isaiah 54:17.) Anybody that blesses you will be blessed. (See the covenant between Abraham and God in Genesis 12.) All of this is released upon the firstborn male child.

Sometimes I look at my life and I realize the benefits of having a dad, even the benefits of being the firstborn of my father's children. There is a time that comes to us that we must understand that the Lord God desires great things for us. Since I have been born again I have been blessed by my heavenly Father. During my life my natural dad has touched and influenced me greatly. I can see that through the characters of the Bible, men and women increase because of the input of a father.

We can see Esau took this whole birthright situation rather lackadaisically:

> And Jacob said, Sell me this day thy birthright. And Esau said, Behold, I am at the point to die: and what profit shall this birthright do to me? And Jacob said, Swear to me this day; and he sware unto him: and he

sold his birthright unto Jacob.

—GENESIS 25:31–33

Why did Jacob press him so much for the birthright? Jacob knew the importance of the firstborn birthright position and the blessing that could be released onto him spiritually. He knew this blessing would cause him to be launched into supernatural realms in God, both on earth and in the spiritual realm. This is why the Bible says Jacob was a prince with God and with men (Gen. 32:28). God puts you in a position where your birthright manifests in you spiritually to take on a roll.

Esau took a carnal position. Because of his hunger, he did not want to waste time arguing over his birthright. Of course he was not going to die from missing a meal or two. His lack of concern for keeping his birthright shows us he did not have a passion to hold on to something of such great importance. He releases it to his brother, Jacob. Esau just gives it right up. There was no desire, pressing, or pull in his spirit to hold on to this precious gift.

The father passed the blessing on to Jacob. Even though Jacob received it through deception, the blessing was still manifested. Isaac put his hand on his son Jacob and blessed him, and a series of unfolding greatness began to come upon him.

First Chronicles 5:2 says, "For Judah prevailed above his brethren, and of him came the chief ruler; but the birthright was Joseph's." Now this is really the key: Judah was great, he prevailed and succeeded in what he put his hands to. He showed the greatness of God by what God did through him. Judah succeeded and did well, even being the fourth child of Jacob.

The firstborn birthrights fell to Joseph. This is apparent by the way Jacob interacted with Joseph. He made him a special coat of many colors and he was attentive to this child that Rachel had born him. Jacob had a passion for the boy, Joseph. It says in 1 Chronicles 5:2, "But the birthright was Joseph's." Joseph delivers Israel, his brothers bow down to him both physically and spiritually. He is not the first-born, but he has the rights because they have been given to him, they have been bestowed upon him by his daddy and by God.

Father God blessed Joseph, but also his natural father, who was also his spiritual father, blessed him. This put Joseph in a position of greatness where he was the ruler. If there was no Joseph, Israel would have been swallowed up and would have vanished from the face of the earth. But God used Joseph to be an instrument of deliverance for Israel. This could occur because God placed on him the firstborn birthright anointing.

This anointing brought Joseph to a place of greatness beyond his years. Joseph would dream of his brothers being in submission to him. These dreams were the result of his spirit recognizing he was greater than he already seemed to be to most people. His birthright was manifested in his spirit. This manifestation comes about by the father laying his hands on his child, and speaking the birthright blessing over him/her. The blessing does not go into the child's flesh, though he is touching the natural body; nor does it enter the soul, though emotions may be shaken by it; rather it is released and imparted into the child's spirit.

Hebrews 12:16 says, "Lest there be any fornicator, or profane person, as Esau, who for one morsel of meat sold his birthright." God says we have to be careful with the birthright blessing. We just cannot take it lightly. Some people may just want to throw it away because they are hungry, they have a sexual issue, or maybe they have a mental problem. They refuse to pull it to their bosom and embrace it properly.

This firstborn birthright issue of the Old Testament was changed by Jesus Christ. The Bible says, "To the general assembly and church of the firstborn, which are written in heaven, and to God the Judge of all, and to the spirits of just men made perfect" (Heb. 12:23). The shedding of Jesus' blood on the cross gives us all the opportunity to be first-born children of God. Through our belief in Him we become the church of the firstborn with the rights of greatness and blessings. Anyone that curses me will be cursed, and anyone that blesses me will be blessed. Heaven will shine upon me and the goodness of the land will be mine.

Blessings can be released into the lives of every man and woman in the body of Christ who recognize they are part of the firstborn church. As a member of the body of Christ you are not just a number with God. You are God's child. You have taken on an important position. Believing this means you have to recognize that God has released a blessing on you. A blessing of fruitfulness and increase, a blessing of prosperity and anointing, and a blessing of strength and insight that will take you from where you are to new heights, new depths, and new realms in Christ Jesus. God is about to start stretching you and making you greater. Now here's your birthright, but you have to recognize it.

Fathers in the kingdom need to minister to their children by speaking over them a birthright blessing. Do not come up short, dads. Bless your children in word, in deed, and with the laying on of hands. The Word is true.

Looking at the lives of Abraham, Isaac, Jacob, and Joseph we see the sons ended up being greater than the fathers. As great as Abraham was, Isaac was greater. As great as Isaac was, Jacob was greater. Then there was Joseph who received the release of the firstborn right even though he wasn't the firstborn. Joseph was the twelfth child in the lineage of Jacob. He was the eleventh son, but he was the twelfth child. The number twelve is symbolic of government and structure, foundation and strength. This is what God placed in him so He could use Joseph to deliver an entire nation that was on the verge of being wiped out by famine. Joseph was greater than his father in that Joseph became a leader of Egypt. He had the ability to transform the lives of those around him by being a blessing to them.

Joseph's father, from the time of the robe of many colors was blessing his son. Even though there was years of separation, the years of spiritual and natural influence from Jacob to Joseph helped him become who he was. You can become effective in changing your family, your community, your city, and your nation. The Bible says these that turned the world upside down have come here (Acts 17:6). They knew who they were. They were operating in their firstborn/first church birthright position, and they knew that they could change entire cities and countries—the very lives of people.

Ecclesiastes 7:1 says, "A good name is better than precious ointment; and the day of death than the day of one's birth." This is why we tend to pay more attention to Jesus' death than we do His birth. Jesus died and rose from the grave. His death and resurrection is what changes us, not

His incarnation. I celebrate and embrace Jesus' birth, but my salvation does not come from His birth; the change that comes into me takes place at His death and His resurrection.

So, I am part of the firstborn church of Jesus Christ. My birth into this church occurred when I came to salvation and was born again. This was just my beginning. The only one that may really be affected by my initial salvation is me. At the end of my days on earth, the impartations I have received from my father who poured into me, blessed me, called me to be more than what I was, and pushed me to be greater than what he was will speak volumes beyond my birth. This is because the greatness of God was manifested in me. Heaven shone on me all my life and the fatness of the land was released upon me. They that curse me, God will curse; and they that bless me, God will bless.

All of this comes from the impartation of a blessing from my father. The heavenly Father blesses His children, and an earthly/spiritual father blesses his children so they can fulfill the purpose of God in the earth. This fulfilled purpose will make an impact that will change lives in their family and their community. It will continue to bring wave after wave of the glory of God over the lives of others by the presence and the purpose of Jesus Christ in their life. Amen.

Chapter 3

Blessing of a Marriage

MARRIAGE IS A very blessed connection that God allows us to experience as we go forth in life. It is one of many stages that many people pass through. Our society tries to make us believe marriage is less than important. It seems more and more people today would rather live together than get married. They would rather enter into an illegal relationship so they do not have to deal with the responsibilities of marriage. This goes completely against the Word of God.

One thing we have to keep in mind with the blessing of a marriage is a father is an important factor in the marriage blessings. During a traditional marriage ceremony it is normal for the father to come forth with his daughter to present her to her future husband. The officiate says something like: "And who gives this woman to be married to this man?" The father normally responds, "I do." He then kisses his daughter's cheek and releases her to the young man waiting patiently at the altar. Generally in our society the father of the bride pays for the entire wedding ceremony and the reception. Things have changed over the years, and many fathers are not financially able to do this, but in times past it was definitely the case.

In some societies dowries would be given along with

the bride. These would have been either a large lump sum of cash, livestock, clothing, perhaps even machinery. Sometimes the dowry had to be given by the groom-to-be before the daughter would be given to him as his wife. The point is, in all of these situations the father was always very visible, important, and very much involved. In most instances the daddy was powerful and authoritative in demonstrating his role in the marriage ceremony. What people need to realize is that there is a marriage blessing released by a daddy in a marriage ceremony, whether by involvement, word, or deed.

The act of Abraham's giving direction to his servant to get the wife for his son shows Abraham's concern and desire for his son's life and marriage to be blessed.

Let's look at an interesting marriage scenario from the Bible:

> And Abraham was old, and well stricken in age: and the LORD had blessed Abraham in all things. And Abraham said unto his eldest servant of his house, that ruled over all that he had, Put, I pray thee, thy hand under my thigh: And I will make thee swear by the LORD, the God of heaven, and the God of the earth, that thou shalt not take a wife unto my son of the daughters of the Canaanites, among whom I dwell: But thou shalt go into my country, and to my kindred, and take a wife unto my son Isaac.
>
> —GENESIS 24:1–4

Abraham makes his servant, a gentleman by the name of Eliezer, make a promise to him. He says, "Eliezer, I want you to get my son a wife." From the beginning Abraham is involved in the marriage connection of his son, Isaac.

He's practicing one of the future commands of Paul, who warned the Corinthians to "be ye not unequally yoked together with unbelievers" (2 Cor. 6:14). We do not want to give our godly son to ungodly women or our godly daughter to ungodly men. Sometimes there is a lot of compromise in this area. When this happens the father needs to come in and put his foot down, make his statements, and make himself visible.

Abraham tells his servant to get a wife for Isaac from his people in his land. This can be interpreted for us as "from the church" or "from the believers in the house of God." I do not want my son to marry just anyone off the street. I do not want him to marry an unsaved woman; I do not want him to marry a religious woman; I do not want him to marry a woman that is on drugs; and I do not want him to marry a loose or sexually promiscuous woman. I want my son to marry someone from the house of God, a child of God, someone who has been washed in the blood of Jesus and is walking in the ways of the Word of the Living God. The ungodly union makes us one flesh even in the ungodly realm. God calls us to not be joined spiritually and naturally with the wrong person (1 Cor. 6:16; 2 Cor. 6:14). We do not want to have a false balance; there should be no unequal yoking (Prov. 11:1).

Abraham sends his servant on a journey to the land where he hopes he will find the blessed wife for his son. Genesis 24:33 says, "And there was set meat before him to eat: but he said, I will not eat, until I have told mine errand." Eliezer was on his way to find this wonderful wife for Isaac, the son of Abraham, but I find something interesting in that he refused to eat. Eliezer knew that finding the right woman was a deep spiritual issue, and he had gone on a fast. There are spiritual, covenantal boundaries for family ties that must be embraced when arranging a holy union before God. Eliezer knew this and refused even to eat before he got everything settled for his master's son.

Eliezer also knew the importance of allowing God to be in control of the situation. He spent time in prayer and trusted God to give him a sign as to which woman was the right one. He needed a confirmation from God, and I think that we all could use confirmations in our daily decision-making. Eliezer prayed that the future wife of Isaac would draw water from the well for him and his camels. Rebekah came along and was a complete answer to his prayers. Eliezer says:

> And before I had done speaking in mine heart, behold, Rebekah came forth with her pitcher on her shoulder; and she went down unto the well, and drew water: and I said unto her, Let me drink, I pray thee. And she made haste, and let down her pitcher from her shoulder, and said, Drink, and I will give thy camels drink also.
> —Genesis 24:45–46

In this story, Eliezer represents the movement of the Holy Spirit. The Holy Spirit will bear witness and set boundaries for the right person to wed your son or your daughter, so the union is godly, holy, and powerful; not twisted and perverted. Today nearly sixty percent of all marriages end in divorce. We do not want our children to be a part of that statistic. We want them to be a part of the other forty percent; where "what therefore God hath joined together, let not man put asunder" (Matt. 19:6). When God brings two people together in marriage they will be together until the end of their lives on earth. When you trust the Holy Spirit to bring the perfect spouse for your child remember how Eliezer handled the situation: he did not do anything until he saw her coming; he went forth in his operation according to his prayer, he began to see her minister to him and his camels and this helped him to know she was the one.

> Then Laban and Bethuel answered and said, The thing proceedeth from the LORD: we cannot speak unto thee bad or good. Behold, Rebekah is before thee, take her, and go, and let her be thy master's son's wife, as the LORD hath spoken.
>
> —GENESIS 24:50–51

Rebekah's family believed God had orchestrated her meeting Abraham's servant. They said that they could not speak good or evil about the situation because it was God's will. You see when it is handled properly, it is God. We should not allow our children to marry out of lust, power, or greed—we should encourage them to marry out of God's will. With this we can speak neither good nor evil—it is just God.

Laban and Bethuel told Eliezer to take Rebekah away to his master's son. This is a wonderful movement of the Lord. Rebekah had never seen Isaac and Isaac had never seen Rebekah, though when they see each other for the first time they immediately come together. Rebekah sees Isaac in the field, and she begins to prepare herself. When she comes to him, he takes her into his mother's tent where he's dwelling and they join themselves in the union of marriage. (See Genesis 24:62–67.)

Let's move on in our discussion of marriage. John 2:1 says, "And the third day there was a marriage in Cana of

Galilee; and the mother of Jesus was there." At this wedding Jesus performs his first miracle: He turns water into wine. In this story the red color of the wine represents the blood of Jesus being applied to the marriage. Even if the wine was a deep purple, it represents the royalty of King Jesus and godliness being applied to the union. Wine brings joy. It is also symbolic of the movement of the Holy Ghost as new wine, which Jesus says He will give to us. (See John 14:26.) The men who are drunk with wine at the wedding feast are symbolic of the outpouring of the Holy Ghost at Pentecost. (See Acts 2:4, 13.)

A marriage should be a miracle; the joining of two lives, two hearts, two families. Abraham was perhaps the first father to get involved in this process. He knew there was a need for him to be involved in the future of his son and in the blessing of his son's marriage. Fathers: be involved in the process of your children getting married. Children: allow your father to guide and direct your steps as decide who to wed. If your natural father is not around, or is not a Christian, let your spiritual father be involved in guiding you to pick the spouse your heavenly Father has planned for your life, so your marriage will be blessed. Your spiritual father may be your pastor, apostle, or bishop, or some other spiritual mentor you can trust. Let this person be involved. Even if he's handling the wedding ceremony, let him have his say in the choice of spouse.

God blesses the union of Isaac and Rebekah because Abraham was involved in the union, and he believed a miracle would take place. Isaac came to be even greater than Abraham. God is going to do something supernatural in the marriages of your children, by His Spirit and by His power. A miracle will take place.

The Bible says the wedding in Cana took place on the third day. (See John 2:1.) Jesus repeatedly told His disciples He would rise from the grave on the third day. (See Matthew 17:23, 20:19; Mark 9:31, 10:34; Luke 9:22, 18:33, 24:7.) This resurrection power in a wedding ceremony or union is the resurrected presence of God; it is a restorative, rejuvenating, and regenerating presence.

The father of the bride has to be praying over and blessing his daughter. He also is making a commitment in the physical act of giving her away and in the financial aspect of financing the ceremony. These things are necessary for the launching of prosperity and blessings in his daughter's future life. The young man that takes a woman without her father's release is going to be met with trouble in the days to come. He needs the woman's father to release her into his arms with blessings and declarations of the goodness of the Lord for their future life together.

> Let brotherly love continue. Be not forgetful to entertain strangers: for thereby some have entertained angels unaware. Remember them that are in bonds, as bound with them; and them which suffer adversity, as being yourselves also in the body. Marriage is honourable in all, and the bed undefiled: but whoremongers and adulterers God will judge.
>
> —HEBREWS 13:1–4

According to this passage, marriage is honorable; it is not a shame to get married, and it is not a sign of weakness to wed. This is great. God honors and blesses your union. He blesses the blessing of the father upon the involvement of the union. God honors and blesses the union of the young man to the young woman as they come together.

God blesses and honors the union.

The second thing God does is bless the union in all realms of life. This means the couple is blessed physically, spiritually, emotionally, financially, mentally, etc. He blesses them with children. In truth, what God is really doing is blessing the couple with the blessings he released upon Adam and Eve. In blessing them, God said, "Be fruitful, and multiply, and replenish the earth, and subdue it: and have dominion over the fish of the sea, and over the fowl of the air, and over every living thing that moveth upon the earth" (Gen. 1:28). These words begin to manifest in the marriage of two people when their union is blessed by a father. Father God brought Adam and Eve together. Father Abraham was involved in the joining of Isaac and Rebekah. Likewise, fathers today need to be involved in the marriage process of young men and young women to bring them to the next level of maturity.

Fathers need to be vocal. The Bible says, "So then he that giveth her in marriage doeth well; but he that giveth her not in marriage doeth better" (1 Cor. 7:38). Now that is really wild. What God is saying is it is good for a man to give his daughter in marriage. God's going to bless the union. But it is better if the father does not give her if he sees something is wrong with the man she desires to marry. If the young man is abusive, does not have a job, or simply is not a born-again believer in Christ Jesus, the father does better if he refuses to give his daughter away to him.

The influence and the importance of the position of that father are very necessary to the operation and the flowing of that marriage. Daddy says yes, there's a blessing. Daddy says no, there's a blessing. Abraham said, *Yes, go get for my son a wife from a godly environment; let's bring them together that fruit might come forth in their life physically, spiritually, mentally, and financially.* The daddy's blessing from the beginning of that marriage is going to take that marriage far into the future. Young people, make sure your fathers are involved in your marriage affair. Dads, make sure you are involved in the marriage affairs of your children. If you do this, Father God will make sure a blessing is released from heaven into the union just as Jesus did at the marriage in Cana. A miracle is going to manifest in that gathering. Amen.

Chapter 4

Blessing of a Father on Ministry

THE IMPORTANCE OF the input of a spiritual father in the lives of ministers and those in ministry (male and female alike) is so important. It helps to project and accelerate us beyond where we are. Sometimes, because we are trying to do things on our own ability, we run into oppositions, delays, and detours. These troubles could completely be avoided if someone was there just to push us or give us some instruction and insight. There are incidents in the Word of God regarding the blessing of ministers, as well as accounts of people who were coming into ministry being blessed and/or encouraged by their spiritual fathers.

> And it came to pass, when they were gone over, that Elijah said unto Elisha, Ask what I shall do for thee, before I be away from thee. And Elisha said, I pray thee, let a double portion of thy spirit be upon me. [The spirit he's referring to is not the Holy Spirit—capital "S"—it is the spirit of man—small "s."] And he said, Thou hast asked a hard thing: nevertheless, if thou see me when I am taken from thee, it shall be so unto thee; but if not, it shall not be so. And it came to pass, as they still went on, and talked, that, behold, there appeared a chariot of fire, and horses of fire, and parted them both asunder; and Elijah went

up by a whirlwind into heaven. And Elisha saw it, and he cried, My father, my father, the chariot of Israel, and the horsemen thereof. And he saw him no more: and he took hold of his own clothes, and rent them in two pieces. He took up also the mantle of Elijah that fell from him, and went back and stood by the bank of Jordan.

—2 KINGS 2:9–13

Elisha was not so much a prophet as he was a farmer and a herdsman. He left his home and natural parents to follow Elijah, a prophet of Israel. Elijah became Elisha's spiritual father. In verse 12 we hear him cry out, "My father, my father," referring to Elijah. There was a link between these two men. A strong father/child relationship is something we all probably desire. A good father looks out for your best interests. He's not there to take advantage of you, downgrade you, or abuse you. He's looking out for your best portion of life; he wants to see your betterment.

In the process of this Elisha sees Elijah taken up after they had discussed the fact that Elisha wanted a double portion of Elijah's spirit. You have probably heard the expression, "I am twice the man that you are." Elisha wanted to be twice the spiritual man Elijah was. His desire was to be greater than his daddy. Every son and daughter should want to be greater than their spiritual parents.

After Elisha sees Elijah taken, he picks up the mantle. The mantle is the connection for his greatness. With the mantle in his possession Elisha performs his first miracle: he parts the Jordan. (See 2 Kings 2:13–14.) Based on the scriptural information given on Elisha, we see that he did more than double the amount of miracles Elijah did. He indeed became greater. Though Elijah made such a heavy impact in Israel, Elisha was now greater than his father. What a supernatural wonder! We must remember that only God could perform such a supernatural feat. It was a blessing; it is mind-blowing and earthshaking that a man could submit his life to another man so completely. Because Elisha embraced the fathering of Elijah, Elisha was able to become twice as effective as Elijah in serving God.

Many of us miss out on the blessing of ministry. I want to be projected, accelerated, and sent forth in the Spirit into the future God has planned for me. I can do this by submitting to my spiritual father. He is able to bless me, which will elevate me to new heights and new realms in the Spirit. When there is a true link between a father in the kingdom and his children, the father has the ability to release and impart his spirit to his children and project them further along. At the same time, there's a need for me to work on my own anointing by seeking God's face. Each individual needs to get into the presence of God.

There's an impartation, anointing, and a blessing that can come to spiritual sons and daughters from their spiritual fathers to accelerate them in ministry. Elijah's primary son, the one who washed Elijah's hands, embraced him, and stayed as close as he could, was Elisha, and he gained the impartation of the father. That is why we need true fathers; not fathers who are compromising or who act in an ungodly manner, but fathers who are concerned about the well-being of their children. If I am going to call a man a father, then I expect him to bring an increasing and a blessing by the Spirit of the Lord into my life, not destruction. We do not need fathers who take advantage of their children, who try to do sexual evil towards them, or who try to harm them financially. We do not need fathers who try to manipulate and control their spiritual children by filling them with fear.

> And the LORD said unto Moses, Gather unto me seventy men of the elders of Israel, whom thou knowest to be the elders of the people, and officers over them; and bring them unto the tabernacle of the congregation, that they may stand there with thee. And I will come down and talk with thee there: and I will take of the spirit which is upon thee [small "s" again, the spirit of a man], and will put it upon them; and they shall bear the burden of the people with thee, that thou bear it not thyself alone.... And Moses went out, and told the people the words of the LORD, and gathered the seventy men of the elders of the people, and set them round about the tabernacle. And the LORD came down in a cloud, and spake unto him, and took of the spirit that was upon him, and gave it unto the seventy elders: and it came to pass, that, when the spirit rested upon them, they prophesied, and did not cease.
>
> —NUMBERS 11:16–17, 24–25

The only one prophesying during this move was Moses, Aaron and Miriam; the primary prophet of course was Moses. Now Moses is prophesying powerfully, tremendously and earth-shaking prophetic volumes, but he needed help. He's counseling, prophesying, and ministering to the multitude of Israel daily. This is draining work. He receives council from his father-in-law, who says, "Moses, you are going to kill yourself if you continue like this." So under the instruction of God Moses brings his sons into the tabernacle. There were no women present because the nation of Israel was a predominately male-oriented society. We even see that same male-oriented culture affecting church life in the New Testament. God, however, has never been male-oriented. In Genesis it states, "Male and female created he them; and blessed them" (Gen. 5:2). God has always been looking to bless the man and bless the woman. That is why we have prophetesses in the Word like Miriam and Deborah.

Looking back at the passage from Numbers, out of the seventy men the anointing only falls on sixty-eight of them. They begin to prophesy and speak the word of God, but two of them were not there, they "had remained in the camp." Even though they were not at the gathering of the elders "the Spirit also rested on them, and they prophesied in the camp" (Num. 11:26, NIV). A young man comes running from the camp and says to Moses, "We have a problem in the camp; the two elders that missed the meeting are prophesying!" (See Numbers 11:27.) It did not matter if they were at the gathering or not; God had determined He was going to put the spirit of Moses on all seventy.

Your prophetic ability will increase if your father moves prophetically. Your knowledge of revelation of the Word will increase if your father is a revelatory preacher. Your miracle ministry, healing ministry, discernment, spiritual gifts, and faith level will increase as your father releases his spirit upon you. I am not talking about our heavenly Father now, who is always involved in our lives. I am speaking of your spiritual father who walks in this earth realm. As he releases his anointing upon your life it takes you higher to make you greater than what you are.

The full impact of the mantle of Moses is eventually released upon Joshua, who supersedes Moses. Moses takes the Israelites through the wilderness and brings them to the Promised Land, but he never actually gets to enter it. Joshua is the one who physically takes the Israelites into the Promised Land. With him the Israelites take possession of this territory. The powerful impact of God in this whole situation is fearsome. Here is the Lord moving forward by His spirit, His presence, His anointing, His joy and His love. God moves forward to raise up an eldership for Israel by releasing the spirit of Moses upon the leaders. Here he is blessing the ministry of others that their ministry might go higher and further than his own.

> Moses therefore wrote this song the same day, and taught it the children of Israel. And he gave Joshua the son of Nun a charge, and said, Be strong and of a good courage: for thou shalt bring the children of Israel into the land which I sware unto them: and I will be with thee.
>
> —DEUTERONOMY 31:22–23

Now here is an interesting thought: when Moses tells Joshua, "I will be with thee," is he talking of God or himself? My answer is twofold. God is with you because He promises "I will never leave thee, nor forsake thee" (Heb. 13:5). I believe God was going to release the anointing and ministry of Moses onto Joshua so Joshua could take the Israelites to the next level. As Israel takes over the Promised Land, the ministry of the elders is taken to the next level; it is taken higher and further and makes an impact in the earth realm. Secondly, I believe the spirit of Moses coming upon Joshua is a demonstration of the same principle that played out between Elijah and Elisha. The spirit of one man came upon another man and took him to a new height. I believe that is the same way God wants to pour out and release anointing from fathers in the kingdom upon their spiritual children so that their ministries may be blessed.

Moses and Joshua have a series of meetings in the presence of the congregation of Israel. During these meeting Moses keeps repeating to Joshua the things that God had told him. Moses never really tells Joshua, "You'll do something different than I did." He repeats and releases to Joshua what was given to him. In turn, Joshua embraces the revelation of his father, and whatever God wants to add on later, He could. Joshua was actually taking up the baton, or mantle, of Moses and running forward.

Every man of God and every woman of God needs a spiritual daddy. Paul says there are thousands of teachers and instructors, but there are few fathers (1 Cor. 4:15). As it is in the natural so it is in the spirit. There is a shortage of spiritual fathers. Nevertheless, every believer needs a father—or mother—in the Lord. There might be other fathers and mothers who speak into your life, but just like you had one daddy in the natural and one mommy in the natural, so do you have one spiritual father or mother in the kingdom. You may have other fathers give you instruction, but there is one true father in the Lord for you, and he has the spiritual authority to cause your ministry to go from where it is to being a hundredfold greater. Paul did this with his spiritual son Timothy. Paul poured his spirit into Timothy.

If you do not have a spiritual father, you need to get one that can make an impact in your life and bless your ministry. We all should want our ministry blessed by a father in the kingdom of God. Blessings help you to avoid certain controversies, detours, disruptions, and abrupt disturbances. In turn they enable you to leap forward into a spiritual future of greatness so that you can do even greater exploits for God than your daddy did. That is what God wants for us: to go from glory to glory to glory.

Chapter 5

Getting Sent Forth Blessing

So far we have touched on different areas such as marriage and ministry. Now we are going to talk about going forth. This means whatever I do going into college I need a blessing, when I decide to get married I need a blessing, when I choose a direction of business I need a blessing, if I am going to relocate to a different part of the world I need a blessing. In order to go forth in anything, you need a blessing on your life.

I believe the word, instruction, direction, encouragement, and blessing of a father is strongly needed in a child's life. There is one passage from the Bible that really illustrates this for me. Let's look at together:

> Except the LORD build the house, they labour in vain that build it: except the LORD keep the city, the watchman waketh but in vain. It is vain for you to rise up early, to sit up late, to eat the bread of sorrows: for so he giveth his beloved sleep. Lo, children are an heritage of the LORD: and the fruit of the womb is his reward. As arrows are in the hand of a mighty man; so are children of the youth. Happy is the man that hath his quiver full of them: they shall not be ashamed, but they shall speak with the enemies in the gate.
>
> —PSALM 127

I believe God is going to build the city, and that is you. God uses daddies to help to build you with instruction and encouragement. I believe a daddy really has to be an encourager, telling you that you are doing well. He needs to build you up, establish the city that you are, and the house that you are. He needs to help you build it properly so you can be sure of who you are. The sending forth blessing is to help you acknowledge who you are so you can get to your place in God.

Sometimes we are trying to function with a lack of sleep. We rise up early, and go down late. We do not sleep well because we feel insecurity over what the future holds. A father should be releasing blessings on his children letting them know their future is great. He should speak positive blessings over them like: you are going to be prosperous; you are going to be successful; you are not going under, you are going over; you are not going down, you are going up, you are not the tail, you are the head; you are not a failure, you are successful. A father needs to be pouring into the spiritual/natural child information and understanding so that he understands the role and purpose of the father in his life. This way the child can be everything he is supposed to be and succeed and go forth into the blessing of the Lord by being blessed and sent forth.

It is exciting for a man of God when he understands his role as a father. Having children is a reward for him that he has to handle very preciously. The Bible says, "Children are an heritage of the LORD: and the fruit of the womb is his reward" (v. 3). A father always wants to see his children do well. In Scripture, the true essence of a father is he is always developing his children and blessing them and sending them forth so they will do better than he did in life. This is because every father wants his son or daughter to be greater than he is. This is one of the main purposes of sending people forth. You are not sending them forth so they come back struggling; you are sending them forth so they become greater in God than what they are already. You are sending them forth so their greatness is manifested in the earth in a large capacity. You are sending them forth for that purpose. This is also a reward for you, because the greater your children become the more successful you realize you have become yourself. Your children are your legacy here on the earth.

The passage continues that children are "as arrows are in the hand of a mighty man" (v. 4). Thinking about shooting a bow and arrow, consider this: when you send your child forth you want to send them in the right direction. I had the opportunity to shoot a bow and arrow once on my honeymoon with my blessed wife, Pastor Gayle. I guess from watching Robin Hood and other medieval-type movies I just thought that you grabbed the bow, put the arrow in, pulled and let it fly. So I took the bow and arrow in my hand and pulled it. The instructor said, "Shoot at that balloon." I said, "Come on." I pulled the bow back as far as I was able to get it and released it. The arrow never even reached the target. The instructor looked at me and said, "See, it looks easier than it is. You have got to pull that bow back until you can either feel it or hear it pop. If you want to get more power behind it, you have got to pull it back until you feel that pop again." As I began to pull it back again, I realized how difficult it was. At that moment I began to feel pressure and tension in my arms, my chest, and my neck as I pulled that bow. I did get it to the first pop, and I pulled it a little bit more with the best of my ability to tighten that arrow. This time when I released it the arrow hit the target. It did not hit the balloon, did not come anywhere near the bull's-eye, but it hit the target.

From this experience I definitely learned the difficulty of launching or sending forth one's spiritual children to fulfill God's perfect will in their lives. There is pressure involved, difficulty involved, and if a father is doing what he should be, he will always direct his child toward the bull's-eye. The method the father uses may not always be appreciated. The way that he handles himself may not always be well digested, but the purpose is to get that arrow to the bull's-eye. He should not just try to his the target, but he should aim to get his child to that bull's-eye. He wants that child to hit the mark, not just once in their life but many times. It takes a mighty man to keep pulling on that bow. A father needs to be a mighty man.

A father should also be a gatekeeper in his city. The Bible says he talks with the enemy in the gates (v. 5). A father should be making preparation and position for his children: physically, spiritually, emotionally, and financially. It is a brand new day! New direction completely changes the course of everything. It can cause the lives of others to be changed so that they become greater than what they are already.

Finally, the main point of this psalm is that there should be happiness in a man that has many children. A man should be happy if he has a quiver full of children. There is controversy about how many arrows it takes to fill a quiver: five, six, or eight arrows. Obviously it depends upon the size of the quiver. But regardless of how many spiritual children you have—five, six, eight, fifty, or five thousand—launch them all! I assume the natural and spiritual run parallel. If you cannot properly care for a large number of children in the natural, then do not have them. Have one or two, be happy, and go on with your life. But if you can care for ten, go ahead and have them if that is what you desire.

The same holds true with spiritual children. You shouldn't boast that you have "all these spiritual children," and their lives are going haywire and failing. You want your spiritual children to be more successful than you are. So take as many spiritual children as you have and launch all of them; not towards the target, but towards the bull's-eye.

Throughout Scripture, fathers sat at the gates of the cities. To get a spot at the gate of the city you had to be a powerful man, a head of a home, or set up your own institution; you had to be a mighty man, a valiant man, a hero, famous in the realms of your home, successful in the city, have a voice naturally, spiritually, emotionally, mentally, or financially. If you had a spot, you were one of the fathers. The end of Psalm 127 says tells us that we want our children to be able to deal with the enemies at the gate. The only way my children are going to be able to deal with the enemies at the gates of the city (gate of their life, gate of their business, gate of their finance, gate of their home, gate of their community) is that I have already sent them forth with a blessing. I am expecting them to be the greatest thing here on earth. The joy of a daddy is to know that his children are, or one day will be, greater than he is and accomplish things that he never did. That is where a father finds joy and that is the purpose of him releasing the blessings of sending them forth.

A sent forth blessing means that you go out into the fields of life, go out in the direction of this world, and succeed to the utmost in what you put your hand to. This is because daddy blessed you and sent you out, with not a curse on his lips or a discouraging word from his mouth, but with faith in his heart and a blessed word in his mouth. That word gave you life to succeed in all that you try to do.

Chapter 6

Restoration Blessing

I BELIEVE THIS IS a very important area of blessing for the body of Christ, especially for individuals under the anointing of the Holy Ghost. This desire behind this blessing is for the Spirit of the Lord to bring restoration to the lives, ministries, hearts, and minds of the children of God. I believe a father also has a big part in bringing this restoration. Restoring is a big responsibility for fathers.

In general, a person, whether a grown person in the kingdom of God or a young person still living with their natural mother and father, does not want to fail mommy and daddy. They do not want daddy to feel they are a failure. A father needs to have the love and the ability to restore a lost child to Christ. Some children seem to stray from their faith, or they have issues they need to deal with. A father needs to restore them through the anointing of the Holy Spirit, not beat them down while their in the turmoil of life.

> A certain man had two sons: And the younger of them said to his father, Father, give me the portion of goods that falleth to me. And he divided unto them his living. And not many days after the younger son gathered all together, and took his journey into a far country, and there wasted his substance with riotous living. And when he had spent all, there arose a

mighty famine in that land; and he began to be in want.

—LUKE 15:11–14

The father in this story does not seem to challenge his youngest son's desire at all. The son felt it was his time. He comes to his father and asks him to give him his inheritance and send him forth. He says to his father, "Do not you have something for me?" "Yes, I guess I do as your dad," the father replies. A father should have an inheritance set aside for his children. The Bible says he should leave something for his children (Prov. 13:22; 2 Cor. 12:14). So the father comes and gives it to him. The son then goes out and quickly finds himself in desperate want; perhaps he lacked knowledge or had the wrong connections, maybe he was in the wrong places at the wrong times, but he loses everything.

> And when he came to himself, he said, How many hired servants of my father's have bread enough and to spare, and I perish with hunger! I will arise and go to my father, and will say unto him, Father; I have sinned against heaven, and before thee, And am no more worthy to be called thy son: make me as one of thy hired servants. And he arose, and came to his father. But when he was yet a great way off, his father saw him, and had compassion, and ran, and fell on his neck, and kissed him.
>
> —LUKE 15:17–20

Now that is the restorative power of a daddy! He did not wait for his son to come in and start groveling, begging, and running through his presentation of "my life's mistakes." I believe this father had been looking out for his boy since the day he left. The father knew his son was not ready to do what he wanted to do. He could have refused to give his son his inheritance early. But he knew the young man's rights, and he gave him what he wanted. When we reach the point of failure, complications, and difficulties in life on of the greatest blessings is that when we realize we have a father we can return to, a father that loves us. We have a father that can help to restore us.

The father saw his son at a great distance, and ran to him, fell on his neck, and kissed him. In Malachi 4:6 it says, "And he shall turn the heart of the fathers to the children, and the heart of the children to their fathers." It did not say the heart of the children first. It says the heart of the fathers first. True fathers want to see their children restored, set up, and made strong. Fathers are looking for their children's progress, and if they have to go after them and chase them to bring them to their rightful position in God, they will. A real daddy does not give up on his seed.

> And the son said unto him, Father, I have sinned against heaven, and in thy sight, and am no more worthy to be called thy son. But the father said to his servants, Bring him the best robe, and put it on him; and put a ring on his hand, and shoes on his feet.
>
> —LUKE 15:21–22

Psalm 23:3 says this: "He restoreth my soul." Now I am sure that that young man's soul needed to be restored as well. The soul is your emotions and your mental makeup. This son's soul must have been broken. He had taken such a great step of faith, or step of pride and arrogance depending on how you look at it, that he would succeed on his own. But it all collapsed around him. However, because his daddy loved him with the help of the Almighty God he restored the emotional and mental well-being of his son. God and his father got him straightened out, situated, organized, made him what he needed to be, and got him back in a position to receive a breakthrough and blessings.

Mark 3:5 says, "And when he had looked round about to them with anger, being grieved for the hardness of their hearts, he saith unto the man, Stretch forth thine hand. And he stretched it out: and his hand was restored whole as the other." Restoration brings you back to where you used to be. Eventually it also takes you beyond your beginnings into greater realms. If you used to have three meals a day, a change of clothes everyday, and were able to drive back and forth to work everyday, when you lose it all, restoration brings you back. Once you are restored you have your three meals again, you got clothes to change into everyday, you have transportation again, and eventually you'll have even more. Increase comes to you.

The father in Luke 15 had two sons. The son that failed was restored to the same level as the son that never left home. Judging their status, you couldn't tell the difference between them. The whole family begins to celebrate when this prodigal son returns. The Bible says, "And they began to be merry" (Luke 15:24). They were merry because they believed that God is a restorer.

No daddy wants to see his child fail, because the greatness of a fathers' true presence is seen by people when they look upon his seed. People think, *He must be great because look at what his seed has done; he must be a powerful man because look what his seed has accomplished.* A father should make up his mind to ensure that his son goes from a "zero" to a "hero," that his daughter goes from the "realm of failure" to the "realm of favor." This causes him and his children to realize they do not have to settle for where they are. They can press forth to where God wants them to be.

Luke 19:8 says the following, "And Zacchaeus stood, and said unto the Lord; Behold, Lord, the half of my goods I give to the poor; and if I have taken any thing from any man by false accusation, I restore him fourfold." Receive two things from this passage: the first is God is going to restore you. It is guaranteed. Anything you have lost has to come back to you. Anything that has been taken from you illegally, spiritually, mentally, emotionally, by mistake, or by wrong directions has to be returned to you. It has to be returned to you! Notice how it says "fourfold." Morning, afternoon, evening, night; winter, spring, summer, fall; north, south, east, west; when you receive restoration, the seasons and times of your life change for the better, for the better! It is no longer evening, it is morning. It is no longer winter, it is spring. It is no longer south, it is now north. No matter what error you have made, even if it was in ministry, God has anointed spiritual fathers who will work you through it to get you back to the plain that He wants you to be on. That is why you always have to find a good father, and hopefully that good father finds you. He should be looking for you. Recognize that your days to come are about to be changed; you are about to be better than you were before.

Greatness is yours, breakthrough is yours, power is yours, it is a new day, a new season, you are going to experience the eruptions and breakthroughs and blessings of God like never before. It is a brand new day. All you have to do is hold on, believe, and receive it. The blessings of the father in your life are not just for today but for every day. If you do not have a daddy, pray that God will show you who he is. He may not be the tallest daddy, might not be the wealthiest daddy, he might not be the most well-known daddy, but your spiritual father can speak some things into your life to help you get from point A to point Z, help you to get from the beginning to the end, and help you when you have done your best or your worst and either way you are falling. That godly spiritual father can be there to pick you up and help you to start again. Today is a new day; your life will never be the same. Believe for the increase. Believe for your blessing of your restoration and it will come; no more lacking but only increasing in the goodness of the Lord God.

Chapter 7

Agreement Between Fathers

THROUGHOUT THIS BOOK we have discussed the different kinds of blessings that are imparted into the life of a man or a woman by way of their father. In this chapter we will seal the whole book. This chapter will take your mind, body, and most of your spirit to a level where you will never be the same. If you can possess this revelation you will be enlightened and illuminated. This chapter will enlighten you to the power of covenant relationship and agreement between a father and his children. It will invoke and provoke you to go in supernatural realms of breakthroughs of blessings. The following passage in the Word of God brings me to a new realm of enlightenment:

> If my people, which are called by my name, shall humble themselves, and pray, and seek my face, and turn from their wicked ways; then will I hear from heaven, and will forgive their sin, and will heal their land.
>
> —2 CHRONICLES 7:14

This scripture is powerful! It is wonderful. But read on and we find that 2 Chronicles 7:18 says this, "Then will I stablish the throne of thy kingdom, according as I have covenanted with David thy father, saying, There shall not fail thee a man to be ruler in Israel." Three tremendous statements come out of this verse. I call these the "father statements." I will make these very clear as you read. When you understand the blessings that can be released through a godly father into your life and you see this passage it will transform you.

First God says He is going to establish the kingdom, or the work or operation. In my case, that would be Bread of Life Fellowship the World Outreach Center. It would mean taking the gospel around the world, transforming lives, healing hearts, and delivering minds and bodies by the power of Holy Ghost. So that is a tremendous blessing right there. But then the verse goes on to say that God has "covenanted with David thy father." Your heavenly, Abba Father has come into a covenant with the earthly father, David. Your heavenly Father comes into agreement with your earthly, spiritual father. Now that is powerful.

There are two spiritual presences involved here: the presence of our heavenly Father coming into a covenant agreement with our spiritual father here on earth. When I start to think about that I realize the power that God wants to release upon His children here in the earth realm. The blessings a father who is a godly, holy, and spiritual man of God can release are because God comes into a covenant agreement or a blood contract agreement with him. God the Father comes into an agreement by the way of the blood of the cross with the spiritual father here on earth. Once they come into this agreement every one of the children will be a ruler; speaking more simply all the children shall succeed and not fail.

This concept gets me excited and makes me feel sorry

at the same moment. I get excited for every man, woman, boy, and girl that knows who their spiritual father is. I get excited for every man, woman, boy, and girl that understands the power of their spiritual father in their life to take them to new heights. But I feel sad for every man, woman, boy, and girl that does not have a spiritual father here in the earth, or have not submitted to one. The Bible says you cannot help but rule, you must succeed, when your heavenly Father comes into an agreement with your spiritual father here on earth (2 Chron. 7:18; 6:16). When your father here on earth and your Father in heaven agrees for you, you cannot help but succeed. What a powerful declaration, blessings of marriage, blessings of life, blessings of direction of life, blessings in the area of restoration, blessings in the area of forgiveness, all types of blessings being released unto a man or a woman or a boy or a girl who have submitted to a spiritual father here in the earth! Oh! What a wonderful blessing: when I embrace that revelation I cannot help but succeed.

Second Chronicles 6:16 says:

> Now therefore, O Lord God of Israel, keep with thy servant David my father that which thou hast promised him, saying, There shall not fail thee a man in my sight to sit upon the throne of Israel; yet so that thy children take heed to their way to walk in my law, as thou hast walked before me.

This is powerful: "There shall not fail thee a man in my sight upon the throne of Israel." When the heavenly Father agrees with your earthly father, when your heavenly Father comes into agreement with your earthly father, when your heavenly Father comes into covenant relationship, blood of Christ, spiritual contract relationship with your earthly father, the Bible says none shall fail to succeed. You shall be able to reign, rule, and be victorious. You shall be able to overcome!

You will fulfill your destiny here on earth. What a blessing! God will supernaturally come into agreement from His Father position with your father here on earth. When I read that, I start to say to myself, *Look at what the Lord has done; look what the Lord has said He will do.* I start to think of the fact that if God comes into an agreement with me, a father here on earth, I cannot help but bless my children. The only way for me not to bless my children is if my children do not believe.

I am in agreement with God for my son that he has to succeed. I am in agreement with God for my daughter that she has to succeed. I am in agreement with God the Father and He's in agreement with me as a spiritual father to my children. We come into agreement for my children, and they must not only succeed, but they cannot fail and their life will not be cut off before it is time. They will accomplish what they are to do in the earth, in Jesus' name.

God's word says:

> That the LORD may continue his word which he spake concerning me, saying, If thy children take heed to their way, to walk before me in truth with all their heart and with all their soul, there shall not fail thee (said he) a man on the throne of Israel.
>
> —1 KINGS 2:4

According as I have covenanted with David thy father saying, There shall not fail thee a man to be ruler in Israel.

—2 Chronicles 7:18

If a father wants anything, he wants to see his sons and daughters succeed—spiritually, physically, mentally, emotionally, financially—in every way. If we open our hearts and embrace this truth that the heavenly father has come into a spiritual blood covenant agreement with the earthly, godly, holy, spiritual father, then that father could release and deposit a blessing upon his children to the point that anything and everything they desire would be blessed.

Let me encourage you again: if you do not have a father in the Lord, get one. You need the voice of a spiritual man of God whose in a godly father role to speak into the corridors of your life and bring you from where you are to where you are supposed to be. If you can grasp this, you could find yourself headed in a whole new direction. What you need to do is look up, look out, and say, *Where is the spiritual father that I am to have a relationship with?* You have got to keep in mind that your natural father is your father no matter what; his seed is in you. Whether you are doing good or bad, whether you like everything he says or not, he's still your father. However, when you get yourself a father in the Lord, a father in the things of God, he can start declaring blessings over your marriage, blessings over your business, blessings over your life, blessings over your ministry, and blessings over the direction of your life. You cannot help but succeed.

I bless you today myself, as all the words of this book get into your spirit. May the truths of the Word be released in your life and take you to a new realm in the Holy Spirit.

I come into agreement with the heavenly Father as an earthly father for you, and I ask the Lord God to bless your from the top of your head to the bottom of your feet. I pray that He clears your path and gives you the victory that you need by the grace of His only begotten son Jesus Christ. Amen.

Today is a new day. You will never be the same again if you can grab these truths. God has a spiritual father our there for you. Embrace him, understand him, walk with him, and the relationship will project you. It will lift you to a new height and a new realm to make you see the promises and the blessings released through covenant agreement in your life like never before. It is a new day; enjoy it!